Coach Miller's
Guide and Workbook to
LIFE and SUCCESS

Coach Miller's
Guide and Workbook to
LIFE and SUCCESS

By Michael Miller, M.ED., M.S., Ph.D.

Foreword by Rev. Misi Tagaloa, Ph.D.

Introduction by Buzz Williams

PYRAMID PRESS

Copyright © Michael Miller, M.ED., M.S., Ph.D., 2017

All rights reserved. No part of this book, in part or in whole, may be reproduced, transmitted, or utilized, in any form or by any means, electronic or mechanical, including photocopying, recording, or by any information storage and retrieval system, without permission in writing from the publisher, except for brief quotations in critical articles, books and reviews.

International Standard Book Number-10:0-9968935-0-4
International Standard Book Number-13:978-0-9968935-0-3

Pyramid Press Edition 2017

The paper used in this publication meets the minimum requirements of the American National Standard for Permanence of Paper for Printed Library Materials Z39.48-1984

PYRAMID PRESS
9550 South Eastern Avenue • Suite 253
Las Vegas, NV 89123 U.S.A.

info@pyramidpress.net

Nothing in this world can take the place of persistence. Talent will not: nothing is more common than unsuccessful men with talent. Genius will not; unrewarded genius is almost a proverb. Education will not: the world is full of educated derelicts. Persistence and determination alone are omnipotent.

Calvin Coolidge

Dedication

This book is dedicated to Phil Jackson, the most accomplished NBA coach of all-time and an avid reader and student of the how the mind works.

AND

John Wooden, the greatest college coach in any sport. He taught me how to teach and impressed upon me the importance of doing things properly the first time. His attention to details and the art of learning resonates with me and all that I have the opportunity to teach.

The Power of Words

Who told us that lie that sticks and stones may break your bones but words will never hurt you?

Words have great power, the power to tear down or build up.

Words can deeply hurt someone and cause great wounds or enlighten, empower and liberate.

Words are used to create hope and dreams and we need both to achieve great things. Life is almost pointless without hope and dreams that can eventually turn into reality.

Use your words carefully and powerfully.

Coach Michael Miller, M.ED., M.S., Ph.D.

Foreword

By Rev. Misi Tagaloa, Ph.D.

"Who you are in the world,
is how the world occurs for you."

—Rev. Misi Tagaloa, Ph.D.

Whoever you are and your reason for purchasing this book, this was meant to be. Let me say this: you have something special inside you, that when identified, accessed and utilized, can change the world.

If you are not familiar with my work, I pastor a local church in Long Beach, California. It was a response to a call on my heart, affirmed by community, that would not let go. The call was from somewhere in the cosmos, but it had a local cut that kept it real and life giving. While I recognize the need for change in how the faith community captures and shares God's love, the local stream is a Samoan speaking congregation in the middle of a metropolis in the United States.

Our work led to the Tafesilafa'i Festival which occurs on the intersection of who we are and the world in which we live. It takes place during the Summer each year and because you are reading this book, you are contributing to the work and I look forward to welcoming you as my guest to Tafesilafa'i when your travels bring you to these parts.

Foreword

When I read the first draft of Coach Miller's manuscript, I was reminded of one of the attributes of the Samoan community: Words are precious—and because they are priceless, they are to be mete out only during special occasions. If you have been to a formal Samoan gathering, listening is golden, not everyone gets to speak and those with power are often the last to speak. When the occasion warrants it, the leader would say a few words, but if not, an articulate spokesperson ends up doing all the speaking. Such is this book. It is a collection of written aphorisms with a lot of space so you can reflect deeply on the meaning of what Coach Miller had in mind.

Coach Miller is a prolific writer and has accomplished much during his career. We share a deep connection about universal truths, and are always mindful of the need to ground it in a local context. The magic is not just in the written words, but also on where you are grounding it. So read the quotes, reflect deeply on what each word means on the surface, but more importantly how it resonates internally within you. You will come away with deep knowledge of who you are and why you are here.

Soifua ma ia Manuia
[Abundant Life and Blessings]

Misi

Introduction

By Coach Buzz Williams

Coach Mike Miller knows a lot about life and a lot about basketball. I have known him for many years and know that he is devoted to helping the people that he coaches and works with to improve their situation. He has been in coaching since 1982 and has devoted his career to helping the people he coaches to be a success at whatever they do. He has been coach of the year 18 times in 19 years and has won 14 straight conference championships in Junior College, which is a national record.

Coach Miller knows that his role as a coach is to help his players succeed as basketball players, as teammates and also as a person once their playing days are over. **Coach Miller's Guide and Workbook to Life and Success** is a compilation of the many universal truths and life lessons that Coach Miller has learned in over 30 years of coaching. These truisms he has often shared with his players and has practiced in his own life.

One of the realities of being a coach in any sport is that there are so many opportunities to impart your values, your beliefs and your views on success to your players. That opportunity is also afforded to parents, teachers, leaders, managers, aunts, uncles and mentors as well, with reasonable frequency. That is why this book can be so helpful. This book is full of ideas about what it takes to be a success in life. Everywhere I have coached I have focused on creating a strong culture of learning with my teams and getting each player, each coach and each staff member to be laser focused on the concept that we have to get better every single day. It's far easier for those we work with or coach to get better if they hear and internalize important life lessons that cause them to think differently. That is why in any role you have as a coach, a parent, a leader or a manager you are always on the job looking for those "moments" to influence positive change. And it doesn't hurt to know how to keep yourself grounded and inspired either.

    How do people learn? How do people change? My belief is that people change and learn in "moments". These moments are times when the simplest of messages or a quote shared by someone we like, trust and admire can take hold. It's the change moment. It's that moment when the person you are interacting with comes face to face with a new reality and realizes that their thinking needs to change. They come to the realization that without changing the way they think or how they approach things that nothing will improve. Who knows what precedes the realization that something about me isn't what it needs to be or can be? We do know that a crisis often evokes the desire to change. Hitting rock bottom for some is a catalyst for change. In life and in sports losing or dealing with obstacles or set-backs often forceS us to want to get better or change our path. Charlie Jones, one of the great professional speakers of the last fifty years used to say in his audio tapes: "Obstacles are necessary for success. They force us to get better or quit." Many people are ready to change when they have had a setback or suffered a loss. The right word, the right message at that moment can create incredible change. The person that is affected in that way will likely forever refer to that "moment" as an unforgettable life lesson. It's that moment that coaches, mentors and parents live for and one of the more powerful ways they reach people and bring out the best in people.

When those "ready to change" moments happen what role can we play? We can be there with a simple yet powerful life lesson that is appropriate for the situation and will help that person see the world differently. These are the "moments" when people begin to be impacted enough to truly change. None of us change the way we act until we change the way we think. The life lessons in this book may just be the life lesson your player, child, employee or student needs to change the way they think. These life lessons are short, simple, easy to understand and can have tremendous impact if used at the perfect time and in the right situation. As Napoleon was credited with saying, "It's better to be prepared and not have the opportunity than to have the opportunity and not be prepared." Some of the lessons in this book can and will help you shape people's lives if you learn them and use them. And if you read them, study them and think about them they can possibly change your own life.

One of my favorite quotes in Coach Miller's book is, "Your life is unwritten so write a best seller." How many people could see the world differently if they really understood the power of that one sentence? My guess is many people could benefit from learning that lesson from Coach Miller. I also love the advice that implores us to be more self-aware and to take responsibility for our own development. This simple one sentence, "Everyone wants a savior but no one wants to look in the mirror." One of the most challenging parts of leading others is to get them to understand the criticality of being self-aware and taking responsibility for their own development. All development is self-development and if this one phrase can jolt someone into understanding that "if it's to be, it's up to me" as Joel Weldon says then we have taught (or maybe learned) a life lesson that will shape someone's future and lead them to success in whatever they do.

This book is full of lessons that many of us need. As do our players and our children need. If you read this book and only one or two of these lessons impact you or impact those that you lead then it will be a book you will never forget.

How To Use This Guide and Workbook For Success

Coach Miller's Guide and Workbook to Life and Success is filled with wisdom and philosophy much needed for a successful life. What follows is gathered from years of practical study and achievement in coaching and teaching and can be applied to coaching, business, life and relationships of many types and kinds.

This is a workbook and is meant to be used as an interactive exercise in self-improvement as well as an important and valuable learning tool on several levels. Both conscious and subconscious thoughts are real and valuable and both must be utilized and modified for any lasting positive change. The more we learn about the subconscious mind the more we realize the power it holds over us. This power must be realized and utilized for our own betterment and success. Dreams serve as our own personal connection to the subconscious mind.

Much has been written on dreams and the power they have in our lives. Most people have awakened from a dream with their heart pounding and in a sweat, actually thinking they were in a real life situation. In these moments we are often shocked to learn this reality was only a dream. While dreams are not fully understood, they have been a topic of scientific speculation, as well as a subject of philosophical and religious interest throughout time.

As a coach I learned the power of dreams long ago. Dreaming about something is in fact a way to brainwash yourself into doing or accomplishing something. As an example, I have dreamed of championship moments only to have them come true later. This was not an accident. If there is a power in "speaking something" into existence, there is an even greater force in dreaming something into existence. Before you can do anything you have to "dream" it first. Although dreams are usually involuntarily and occur in the mind during certain stages of sleep, this is not always the case. Dreams can be planted in our own subconscious and at times make a creative thought occur to the person or give a sense of needed inspiration for problem solving.

In my 35 years of coaching I have become adept and an expert in motivating, guiding, mentoring and understanding people. One thing all people have in common is that much of their brain and talent goes under utilized. I too suffer from this flawed human condition and have spent many hours trying to overcome this, utilizing therapy, hypnosis, various types of relaxation techniques, education and esoteric study.

I designed this book to inspire and motivate you to achieve your unlocked and unused potential in a simple way. It's time to become a great success in any area you choose. This is achieved in several ways, not the least of which is the power in your subconscious mind.

The words, stories, lessons and aphorisms contained in this book represent differing viewpoints of wisdom from my 35 plus years coaching. These alone are both powerful and valuable for any one interested in achievement. Let's not stop with the words and lessons, that's not enough. The goal is to connect to the subconscious mind and unlock more power to think, learn and teach others. While the information in this book is interesting and motivating, to get the best results please follow the instructions below.

To have the most powerful impact on your brain please follow the 10 step plan as prescribed:

1. Open the book randomly to a page (note: there are no page numbers, there is no order to learning here).
2. Read one page only.
3. Do this before going to sleep.
4. Read the page aloud three times.
5. Close your eyes for a short time.
6. Read the page in silence to yourself three times.
7. Leave the book open to the page next to your bed (remember no page numbers).
8. When you wake up read the page aloud with a pen in your hand.
9. Now draw or write what comes into your conscious mind on the page.
10. Close the book and think about what you learned and try to teach or share this information with three people today.

How To Use This Guide and Workbook For Success

By following this simple plan you will be able to learn more and achieve more than by reading the pages alone. This is what makes this both a guide and a workbook. There is work to do, and it's more than just reading the pages from front to back.

Each lesson and story is meant to be reflected on both consciously and unconsciously. Each page is meant to be a unique learning experience, and in a different order from person to person. Fate will guide you down the path you are meant to be on at this time. Likewise, if you re-read this book at a different time you will have a different experience.

While it can be both fun and tempting to read this book quickly from cover to cover. The lessons within are short but they are powerful and fun. Like potato chips it's hard to read only one page and stop. This is the way you would read any book. This isn't any book it is a "Guide" and "Workbook" for Your Success.

DO THE WORK and STAY IN TOUCH

In the same way a coach would implore a player not to take a short cut, but trust in the process, I implore you to do the work required for your greatest success. I want to coach you to your greatness and look forward to working with you along this journey. When you finish this specific journey please contact me and tell me about it. I want to learn what you learned. Then, together, we can see about the next step toward your ultimate goals. I am ready to be your coach, are you ready to compete and do the work? Remember success is doing your best to become the best YOU can be.

Coach Michael Miller, M.ED., M.S., Ph.D.
info@coachmiller.net

Coach Miller advises, "Find what you love and let it kill you."

Michael Miller, M.ED., M.S., Ph.D.

What you compromise to keep will eventually be lost.

Coach learned that people listen to rich folks and they pray for poor folks.

Michael Miller, M.ED., M.S., Ph.D.

We all live under the same sky, but we all don't have the same horizon.

At times words can be like a monkey holding a loaded gun to it's own head.

Michael Miller, M.ED., M.S., Ph.D.

Coach Miller points out, "Everyone has a plan until you get hit in the mouth."

Is it better to have a superior person in an inferior position than to have an inferior person in a superior position?

Michael Miller, M.ED., M.S., Ph.D.

Coach Miller advises, "If opportunity doesn't knock, build a door."

Coach Miller learned, "The boss is not always right, but he's never wrong".

Michael Miller, M.ED., M.S., Ph.D.

Enthusiasm and perseverance are the most important traits to possess for success.

Coach Miller believes the only thing worse than a liar is a liar and a hypocrite.

Michael Miller, M.ED., M.S., Ph.D.

Coach Miller observed people will follow the leader before they will follow the vision.

Coach Miller's Guide and Workbook to Life and Success

Bad choices make good stories.

Michael Miller, M.ED., M.S., Ph.D.

Once you love somebody you never stop loving them—it's a one way door.

All difficult people describe themselves as being honest.

Michael Miller, M.ED., M.S., Ph.D.

Everyone is lucky but most don't realize it.

Quitting while you're ahead is not the same thing as quitting.

Michael Miller, M.ED., M.S., Ph.D.

Acceptance is when someone knows you're different but treats you the same.

A true friend sees the first tear, catches the second and stops the third.

Michael Miller, M.ED., M.S., Ph.D.

We all need more fresh fruit, sunshine and sex in our lives.

Live your life in vision not in circumstance.

Michael Miller, M.ED., M.S., Ph.D.

Everyone wants a savior but no one wants to look in the mirror.

Often the loudest one in the room is the weakest one in the room.

Michael Miller, M.ED., M.S., Ph.D.

For long term success build bridges not walls.

Don't speak in code and give false meanings.

Michael Miller, M.ED., M.S., Ph.D.

Coach Miller advises people to manage their expectations.

Don't fight with government workers and bureaucrats–they can't be harmed and you will always lose.

Michael Miller, M.ED., M.S., Ph.D.

Choice not chance determines your destiny.

There are only two basic choices in life: you can be bitter or you can get better.

Michael Miller, M.ED., M.S., Ph.D.

Most humans die far more effectively than they live. "Odd," Coach Miller thought.

Coach Miller's Guide and Workbook to Life and Success

Do good manners ruin good food?

Michael Miller, M.ED., M.S., Ph.D.

Is it better to walk alone than with the crowd going in the wrong direction?

Forgiveness does not change the past but it does enlarge the future.

Michael Miller, M.ED., M.S., Ph.D.

Always give more than is asked and take less than deserved.

Time is the only currency that's worth everything. And yet it cost nothing.

Michael Miller, M.ED., M.S., Ph.D.

Coach Miller on genetics: "An apple tree is an apple tree. You can grow apples that are sweeter or bigger but you're never ever going to grow pears."

Coach Miller prides himself in learning something new, traveling the different road, experiencing the unmet adventure and collecting new friends along the way.

Michael Miller, M.ED., M.S., Ph.D.

Who do you know that needs a room full of mirrors so he can be surrounded by winners?

Good friends are like stars–you don't always see them but you know they are there.

Michael Miller, M.ED., M.S., Ph.D.

Often being poor is like a disease. It passes generation to generation.

Beware of the word equality–it's a lie and for losers.

Michael Miller, M.ED., M.S., Ph.D.

Give yourself freedom from want and the freedom to want.

Don't try to figure out life because life can't be figured out.

Michael Miller, M.ED., M.S., Ph.D.

For your mental health and happiness avoid boring people.

Coach Miller believes you should always say what you're going to do then follow through.

Michael Miller, M.ED., M.S., Ph.D.

In business, make doing business with you easy.

Coach Miller believes humans are programmable. Would advertising exist if this wasn't true?

Michael Miller, M.ED., M.S., Ph.D.

Always leave people better than you found them.

Puppies really keep you in the present.

Michael Miller, M.ED., M.S., Ph.D.

Hope is a good thing-maybe the best of things.

Coach Miller's motto is: "Make some money, have some fun and help people along the way."

Michael Miller, M.ED., M.S., Ph.D.

Marriage is not about finding a person who you can live with, it's about finding a person who you can't live without.

If you want to lead the orchestra you must turn your back to the crowd.

Michael Miller, M.ED., M.S., Ph.D.

When you change the way you look at things, the things you look at change.

We were born to win and almost immediately were conditioned to lose.

Michael Miller, M.ED., M.S., Ph.D.

Never make a decision–let the decision make you.

Old men have dreams and young men have visions.

Michael Miller, M.ED., M.S., Ph.D.

Geniuses are almost always branded as crazy.

Coach Miller's Guide and Workbook to Life and Success

THE HARDER YOU WORK THE LUCKIER YOU GET.

Michael Miller, M.ED., M.S., Ph.D.

I love seeing little things done correctly. In my experience that is one of the secrets to success.

When you're in a relationship, all of your vulnerabilities come to the surface.

Michael Miller, M.ED., M.S., Ph.D.

What do you think of the statement: "A kiss is not a contract and a hug is not a commitment?"

Money isn't worth anything unless you spend it.

Michael Miller, M.ED., M.S., Ph.D.

Effort, energy and attitude is not given enough credit...these traits are as important as ability and talent.

Is control the ultimate expression of power?

Michael Miller, M.ED., M.S., Ph.D.

It's a rare gift indeed to bring confidence to people without being arrogant.

MOST PEOPLE DON'T ASK FOR WHAT THEY WANT. Instead they spend time manipulating.

Michael Miller, M.ED., M.S., Ph.D.

Coach Miller learned you can be right or you can be happy. Choose wisely.

Coach learned, "It's always the people that know you the least, that judge you the most. And when you judge another, you do not define them, you define yourself."

Michael Miller, M.ED., M.S., Ph.D.

The quality of our enemies does us honor...or dishonor.

Paranoia has it's own discipline and it's own logic too.

Michael Miller, M.ED., M.S., Ph.D.

What is deemed criminal in one environment can be deemed virtuous in another. The opposite is also true. Is anything inherently good or bad in any action...except what others judge them to possess?

When thinking of talent versus training use examples of art, music or athletics. Although training is important to the talented performer, talent is omnipotent. You will learn this after trying to train an untalented person to play the violin.

Michael Miller, M.ED., M.S., Ph.D.

All living things seek to protect themselves. When the snake bites it is not personal, you stepped on his tail, that's all.

Coach Miller believes pets are vital to health and happiness in life. Often times even the most horrible psychological wounds can be healed through caring for an animal, and receiving its unconditional love in return.

Michael Miller, M.ED., M.S., Ph.D.

Coach Miller believes that training and talent are different qualities which can produce similar outcomes. Coach Miller has observed that talent triumphs training in most cases.
He thinks that a trained talent can outdo anyone.

Coach Miller learned most people cannot be both good AND nice at the same time.

Michael Miller, M.ED., M.S., Ph.D.

Coach Miller believes you should live life looking through the windshield, not through the rearview mirror.

How can one start the next chapter of life if one keeps rereading the last one?

Michael Miller, M.ED., M.S., Ph.D.

Because life can be tough for many people, make the effort to be friendly when you interact with people. It doesn't cost extra to be nice and it may help someone have a better day.

It's best to work hard in silence
and let success make the noise.

Michael Miller, M.ED., M.S., Ph.D.

It is very, very important to remember never to confuse activity with achievement.

Good leadership means people need to be set up to succeed, not set up to fail.

Michael Miller, M.ED., M.S., Ph.D.

Have you ever met someone who lived to place blame on people? Blame placing is a fools' game and is a weak tool to cover for guilt.

Coach Miller realized that people who live in the past live in regret while people who live in the future live in fear. Live in the present, and enjoy every day to the fullest.

Michael Miller, M.ED., M.S., Ph.D.

Money allows a person to impose their own will on society.

Often times people eat with their eyes.

Michael Miller, M.ED., M.S., Ph.D.

Never try to teach a pig to sing. It wastes your time and annoys the pig.

America's favorite breakfast plate of bacon and eggs, can be used to explain the difference between "dedication" and "commitment." The chicken is dedicated, whereas the pig is committed.

Michael Miller, M.ED., M.S., Ph.D.

Coach Miller observed assertive people can come across as more intelligent than those who are more reserved.

A young man who was taken advantage of in a purchase complained about his misfortune. Coach Miller counseled the youngster, "The bad purchase was not a misfortune at all, rather, it was tuition."

Michael Miller, M.ED., M.S., Ph.D.

Listening is an important skill. Most people listen with the intent to reply, not the intent to understand.

Coach Miller has learned to never interrupt an enemy while they are making a mistake.

Michael Miller, M.ED., M.S., Ph.D.

Coach Miller detests liars, and half truths count as lies.

Humans seem to lie for two reasons: they want to make themselves look better than they really are or to protect themselves.

Michael Miller, M.ED., M.S., Ph.D.

Dogs are the only thing in the world that love a person more than they love themselves.

In the kingdom of the blind the one eyed man is king.

Michael Miller, M.ED., M.S., Ph.D.

Never chase money. Do a good job and let money chase you.

Being happy is a decision. People can be as happy as they want to be, if they so choose.

Michael Miller, M.ED., M.S., Ph.D.

Coach Miller has been asked over and over again, "What are the most important qualities one should possess in approaching a daunting task?" Other than normal intelligence and emotional stability the two most important qualities are Persistence and Determination.

The motto is: "I Will Persist Until I Succeed."

The greater a person's sense of guilt, the greater their need to blame others.

Michael Miller, M.ED., M.S., Ph.D.

A man dangling from a cliff will stretch out his hand to his worst enemy.

One can learn a lot about people by the way they handle these three things: a rainy day, lost luggage, and tangled Christmas tree lights.

Michael Miller, M.ED., M.S., Ph.D.

Coach Miller noticed that many people, both wise and foolish, frequently think love and permission are the same.

Coach offers a friendly reminder to people, "Your life is unwritten; so write a best seller."

Michael Miller, M.ED., M.S., Ph.D.

If you are an excellent archer known for great accuracy, you must have a target to shoot at or you will be wasting your great efforts.

Coach Miller has observed good men in bad churches and bad men in good ones.

Michael Miller, M.ED., M.S., Ph.D.

Coach Miller advised a young man who was pondering whether to attempt a rigorous task: "Decide if you want it more than you're afraid of it."

Coach Miller points out for every minute one is angry one loses sixty seconds of happiness.

Michael Miller, M.ED., M.S., Ph.D.

Coach Miller realized long ago there is no such thing as staying the same. If you're not gaining ground, you are losing ground.

Can you learn to see tragedy as an opportunity?

Michael Miller, M.ED., M.S., Ph.D.

You can feed anyone a fifty pound turkey, as long as it's one bite at a time.

Learn to live by the motto: "Anything worth doing is worth doing right."

Michael Miller, M.ED., M.S., Ph.D.

Any man who doesn't follow his emotions is a foolish man.

A person claimed to be a vegan and was afraid of using knives. It was then that Coach Miller made a new rule: "Beware of people of who don't eat meat and won't use knives."

Michael Miller, M.ED., M.S., Ph.D.

Can you make it a habit to compliment three people every day?

Coach Miller realized the things that are attached to Envy and Jealousy can extend all the way to murder.

Michael Miller, M.ED., M.S., Ph.D.

Anything a person practices, either good or bad, one gets good at it.

I will persist until I succeed.

Michael Miller, M.ED., M.S., Ph.D.

Success is doing the best one can do at all times without making excuses.

Learn to be confident without being cocky.

Michael Miller, M.ED., M.S., Ph.D.

Who knew common sense was so uncommon.

Coach advises his friends to never give permanent feelings to a temporary person.

Michael Miller, M.ED., M.S., Ph.D.

Coach says whatever the problem is, the answer is not in the fridge!

Those who can not be a good example will just have to serve as a horrible warning!

Michael Miller, M.ED., M.S., Ph.D.

Beware of FRIENEMIES!–(enemies who pretend to be friends).

A true friend knows all your weaknesses but helps you to bring out your strengths.

Michael Miller, M.ED., M.S., Ph.D.

Go to sleep with a good idea and get up with a great Purpose.

Coach notes that it takes around two years to learn to speak. But it takes a lifetime to learn what NOT to speak.

Michael Miller, M.ED., M.S., Ph.D.

"As you waste your breath complaining about life, someone out there is breathing their last breath," coach Miller told a chronic complainer.

Confidence is the ability to feel beautiful without needing someone to tell you first, but smiling when someone does.

Michael Miller, M.ED., M.S., Ph.D.

Coach Miller respects men of action. Idea men are a dime a dozen.

Coach believes friends are the family that you choose.

Michael Miller, M.ED., M.S., Ph.D.

If you are moving slow, be reminded that slow motion is better than no motion.

Coach Miller thinks there are two kinds of people in the world: Givers and Takers. The takers may eat better, but the givers sleep better.

Michael Miller, M.ED., M.S., Ph.D.

Normal is an illusion. What is normal for the snake is chaos for the mouse.

A good laugh and a long sleep are the two best cures for anything.

Michael Miller, M.ED., M.S., Ph.D.

The error of the past can be the wisdom of the future.

Coach Miller doesn't need a philosophy of life, he has life instead.

Michael Miller, M.ED., M.S., Ph.D.

True Love can be a serious mental disorder.

Forgiveness is important, not because people deserve forgiveness, but because you deserve peace.

Michael Miller, M.ED., M.S., Ph.D.

Because someone is a DRAMA Queen doesn't mean you have to treat them like Royalty!

People were created to be loved. Things were created to be used. The main reason why the world is in chaos is things are being loved and people are being used.

Michael Miller, M.ED., M.S., Ph.D.

I'll try is just a polite way of saying NO!

Coach Miller observed: "drugs rob potential and rot the souls of humans who use them; this is true of nicotine, alcohol and marijuana."

Michael Miller, M.ED., M.S., Ph.D.

It's a fool's game to allow emotions to overpower intellect.

Be yourself. An original is always worth more than a copy.

Michael Miller, M.ED., M.S., Ph.D.

Coach Miller advises people who are in a dilemma very simply; "Do what's best for you."

Coach Miller observed if you were born broke it's not your fault. But if you die broke–blame yourself!

Michael Miller, M.ED., M.S., Ph.D.

Your life is made of two dates and a dash. Make the most of that dash.

Life isn't a straight road. There is a curve called failure, a loop called confusion, speed bumps called friends, red lights called enemies, caution signs called family, and sometimes you have a flat tire called jobs. But if you have a spare called determination, and the engine called perseverance, you'll make it to a place called success!

Michael Miller, M.ED., M.S., Ph.D.

Challenges are what make life interesting, and overcoming them is what makes life meaningful.

Coach has never been to a fortune teller. He believes the best way to predict the future is to create it.

Michael Miller, M.ED., M.S., Ph.D.

Note the variation between a hand out and a hand up.

Coach Miller learned Americans make up only 5% percent of the worlds' population, yet use 80% of the worlds' drugs.

Michael Miller, M.ED., M.S., Ph.D.

The mind can trick you very easily. Coach learned it's important to watch your own thoughts.

Coach Miller believes hugging is good medicine. It transfers energy and gives the hugged person an emotional lift. Hugging is a form of communication. It can say things you don't have words for.

Michael Miller, M.ED., M.S., Ph.D.

The majority is the safe place to be for most people.

Sharing a meal with a person is the second most intimate thing you can do.

Michael Miller, M.ED., M.S., Ph.D.

Amateurs practice until they get it right, while professionals practice until they can't get it wrong.

Rejection isn't all bad–it's just getting to the point.

Michael Miller, M.ED., M.S., Ph.D.

Be mindful never to discuss cheese around a rat or bread around a bird.

A know-it-all accused Coach Miller of being mean. Coach retorted, "There is a difference between being mean and being accurate".

Michael Miller, M.ED., M.S., Ph.D.

All people could take a lesson from the weather. It pays no attention to criticism.

Empty pockets never held anyone back. Only empty heads and empty hearts can do that. What's your excuse? Coach Miller asks of the underachiever.

Michael Miller, M.ED., M.S., Ph.D.

90% of the world doesn't really care about your problems and the other 10% are glad you have them. This really got coach Miller thinking.

Coach Miller's NO EXCUSE RULE: "Make yourself stronger than your excuses."

Michael Miller, M.ED., M.S., Ph.D.

The only difference between a rut and a grave is the depth.

Coach Miller notices humans use patterned machine-like phrases over and over again. These phrases seem to be held on to very preciously. Coach suggests an exercise: Count the number of times each particular phrase is used in a two day period, and then STOP.

Michael Miller, M.ED., M.S., Ph.D.

Coach Miller notes men hold dearly to the concept of "me". The "me" has been created through years of random, blind and unconscious programming. It is the result of luck, genetics and history. It has as much correlation to your real self as freedom does to fascism.

Dogma is a drug and men are Dogma addicts.

Michael Miller, M.ED., M.S., Ph.D.

Coach Miller observed a person who falls and gets back up, is much stronger than a person who never fell.

What comes easy won't last long, and what lasts long won't come easy.

Michael Miller, M.ED., M.S., Ph.D.

Don't waste words on people who deserve silence. Sometimes the most powerful thing one can say is nothing at all.

Coach Miller explained, "You will never know how strong you are until you have to forgive someone who wasn't sorry, and accept that you will never receive an apology.

Michael Miller, M.ED., M.S., Ph.D.

No one is sent by accident to anyone.

What you allow, is what will continue.

Michael Miller, M.ED., M.S., Ph.D.

Coach Miller doesn't have time to worry about those who don't like him. He's too busy loving those who love him.

Be like a river. Touch things lightly or deeply and move along, as life moves along.

Michael Miller, M.ED., M.S., Ph.D.

Rich people stay rich by living like they're broke. And broke people stay broke by living like they're rich.

Do you ever wonder how words like "turnt", "fleek" and "bae" are understood, but most people don't know how to use "you're", "your", "there" or "their" in a sentence?

Michael Miller, M.ED., M.S., Ph.D.

Every morning you have two choices: "Continue to sleep with your dreams, or wake up and chase them."

There is being peaceful. There is being wild. Can we be both at the same time?

Michael Miller, M.ED., M.S., Ph.D.

At the gambling table there are no fathers and sons.

Being broke from paying bills is totally different than being broke from being lazy.

Michael Miller, M.ED., M.S., Ph.D.

You learn more from funerals than you do from weddings.

Effort, energy and enthusiasm, (sometimes confused with attitude), are underrated traits in success.

Michael Miller, M.ED., M.S., Ph.D.

STUPIDITY is the enemy of mankind.

Coach Miller realized that feelings and emotions are conditioned, not real.

Michael Miller, M.ED., M.S., Ph.D.

Coach Miller understands that life is a challenge, no matter where you're at. The degree of feeling upset is the same for the poor kid in Africa looking for a meal or the blue blood in the Hamptons excluded from a social gathering. People are all the same on the inside.

Coach Miller's Guide and Workbook to Life and Success

Coach Miller believes there are some rocks you just don't turn over.

Michael Miller, M.ED., M.S., Ph.D.

Coach Miller believes less information and more intelligence is desired in most cases.

If someone is a handful–that's what you got two hands for.

Michael Miller, M.ED., M.S., Ph.D.

Giving up doesn't always mean you're weak. Sometimes it means you are strong enough to let go.

It's clear that a man with nothing to lose has everything to gain.

Michael Miller, M.ED., M.S., Ph.D.

Many people are afraid to be free. Trees and butterflies are not afraid to be free.

Be more concerned with your character than your reputation. Because character is what you really are, while your reputation is what people think you are.

Michael Miller, M.ED., M.S., Ph.D.

Coach Miller's advise to investors: "Always buy property when you see blood in the streets."

Coach Miller reminded himself that most people who died yesterday had plans for today.

Michael Miller, M.ED., M.S., Ph.D.

Difficult roads often lead to beautiful destinations.

When you are dead, you don't know you are dead. It is difficult only for others. It is the same when you are stupid.

Michael Miller, M.ED., M.S., Ph.D.

Colors are forces of energy and visualizing them helps release their power.

Trusted friendship requires more than association by birth.

Michael Miller, M.ED., M.S., Ph.D.

To have a successful relationship it is important to be as specific as possible with any request. ASK for what you want. Do not expect others to read your mind.

A dream written down with a date becomes a GOAL. A goal broken down into steps becomes a PLAN. A plan backed by ACTION makes your dreams come true.

Michael Miller, M.ED., M.S., Ph.D.

People should be accepted as they really are and enjoyed or avoided on that basis.

Let your words heal, not wound. And be a blessing-be a friend. Take the time to care and to encourage someone.

Michael Miller, M.ED., M.S., Ph.D.

The early bird may get the worm, but the second mouse gets the cheese in the trap!

Coach Miller observed and predicts, "When all the trees have been cut down, when all the animals have been hunted, when all the waters are polluted, when all the air is unsafe to breathe, only then will humans discover they cannot eat money".

Michael Miller, M.ED., M.S., Ph.D.

Coach Miller says, "Ideas without action aren't ideas, they're regrets.

Coach Miller asks: "What do you cry about?" "What do you sing about?" "What do you dream about?"

Michael Miller, M.ED., M.S., Ph.D.

Coach Miller points out that "Sometimes you bet on the horse and sometimes you bet on the jockey."

Coach Miller is obsessed with simplicity. And making things SIMPLE is very, very HARD.

Michael Miller, M.ED., M.S., Ph.D.

People need to stop coming up with logical excuses for illogical behavior.

Actions make words unnecessary.

Michael Miller, M.ED., M.S., Ph.D.

Coach Miller observed that not everyone in the front row is your biggest fan. The biggest hater paid the most for their ticket.

"Loyalty is hard to find. Trust is easy to lose. Actions speak louder than words", thought coach Miller

Michael Miller, M.ED., M.S., Ph.D.

It is better to ask some questions than to know all the answers.

Silence is the most powerful scream, thought coach Miller

Michael Miller, M.ED., M.S., Ph.D.

Three ways to fail at everything in life are:

1) Complain
2) Blame others
3) Be ungrateful

You never think it's going to end, then, it always ends.

Michael Miller, M.ED., M.S., Ph.D.

A bad attitude is like a flat tire until you change it, you're not going to get anywhere.

Coach Miller's Guide and Workbook to Life and Success

A good start is more than half the whole.

Michael Miller, M.ED., M.S., Ph.D.

Be more likely to give than to give in.

Coach Miller's Guide and Workbook to Life and Success

If you're lonely and have some money, BUY some friends.

Michael Miller, M.ED., M.S., Ph.D.

Coach advises, "time is undefeated."

Money speaks a language everyone understands.

Michael Miller, M.ED., M.S., Ph.D.

Coach Miller advises, "No matter how you feel, get up, dress up, show up, and never give up."

Life was meant to be lived backwards to forwards.

Michael Miller, M.ED., M.S., Ph.D.

Coach Miller said, "Searching for happiness is like traveling the world to find your glasses when they're on your forehead."

Anything in life worth doing is worth over doing. Moderation is for cowards.

Michael Miller, M.ED., M.S., Ph.D.

Old friends are the best friends.

The people you have the most uncomfortable moments with are the people you are closest to.

Being uncomfortable builds strength.

Michael Miller, M.ED., M.S., Ph.D.

Be a pineapple. Stand tall, wear a crown, and be sweet on the inside.

Coach Miller has learned it is much wiser to take advice than to give it.